HackneyandJones.com

Writers and Publishers

HACKNEY & JONES

VISIT

HACKNEYANDJONES.COM

NOW

Free fiction books, non-fiction and kids
activity sheets.

BLOG POST TEMPLATE

Title ideas (use keyword research)

Overall point of blog post (to inform, solve a problem, educate, entertain) - give more detail here

What are 3- 5 points that need answering in this blog post (use google, quora, questions from forums etc)

Is there a particular product/s I want to promote or a website I want to send traffic to? Give details of benefits of those products and why it is relevant to this blog post.

What other media/videos/souces/links will I include giving more value to the blog post. Who is an expert in this area? Give details below:

BLOG POST TEMPLATE

Title ideas (use keyword research)

Overall point of blog post (to inform, solve a problem, educate, entertain) - give more detail here

What are 3- 5 points that need answering in this blog post (use google, quora, questions from forums etc)

Is there a particular product/s I want to promote or a website I want to send traffic to? Give details of benefits of those products and why it is relevant to this blog post.

What other media/videos/souces/links will I include giving more value to the blog post. Who is an expert in this area? Give details below:

BLOG POST TEMPLATE

Title ideas (use keyword research)

Overall point of blog post (to inform, solve a problem, educate, entertain) - give more detail here

What are 3- 5 points that need answering in this blog post (use google, quora, questions from forums etc)

Is there a particular product/s I want to promote or a website I want to send traffic to? Give details of benefits of those products and why it is relevant to this blog post.

What other media/videos/souces/links will I include giving more value to the blog post. Who is an expert in this area? Give details below:

BLOG POST TEMPLATE

Title ideas (use keyword research)

Overall point of blog post (to inform, solve a problem, educate, entertain) - give more detail here

What are 3- 5 points that need answering in this blog post (use google, quora, questions from forums etc)

Is there a particular product/s I want to promote or a website I want to send traffic to? Give details of benefits of those products and why it is relevant to this blog post.

What other media/videos/souces/links will I include giving more value to the blog post. Who is an expert in this area? Give details below:

BLOG POST TEMPLATE

Title ideas (use keyword research)

Overall point of blog post (to inform, solve a problem, educate, entertain) - give more detail here

What are 3- 5 points that need answering in this blog post (use google, quora, questions from forums etc)

Is there a particular product/s I want to promote or a website I want to send traffic to? Give details of benefits of those products and why it is relevant to this blog post.

What other media/videos/souces/links will I include giving more value to the blog post. Who is an expert in this area? Give details below:

BLOG POST TEMPLATE

Title ideas (use keyword research)

Overall point of blog post (to inform, solve a problem, educate, entertain) - give more detail here

What are 3- 5 points that need answering in this blog post (use google, quora, questions from forums etc)

Is there a particular product/s I want to promote or a website I want to send traffic to? Give details of benefits of those products and why it is relevant to this blog post.

What other media/videos/souces/links will I include giving more value to the blog post. Who is an expert in this area? Give details below:

BLOG POST TEMPLATE

Title ideas (use keyword research)

Overall point of blog post (to inform, solve a problem, educate, entertain) - give more detail here

What are 3- 5 points that need answering in this blog post (use google, quora, questions from forums etc)

Is there a particular product/s I want to promote or a website I want to send traffic to? Give details of benefits of those products and why it is relevant to this blog post.

What other media/videos/souces/links will I include giving more value to the blog post. Who is an expert in this area? Give details below:

BLOG POST TEMPLATE

Title ideas (use keyword research)

Overall point of blog post (to inform, solve a problem, educate, entertain) - give more detail here

What are 3- 5 points that need answering in this blog post (use google, quora, questions from forums etc)

Is there a particular product/s I want to promote or a website I want to send traffic to? Give details of benefits of those products and why it is relevant to this blog post.

What other media/videos/souces/links will I include giving more value to the blog post. Who is an expert in this area? Give details below:

BLOG POST TEMPLATE

Title ideas (use keyword research)

Overall point of blog post (to inform, solve a problem, educate, entertain) - give more detail here

What are 3- 5 points that need answering in this blog post (use google, quora, questions from forums etc)

Is there a particular product/s I want to promote or a website I want to send traffic to? Give details of benefits of those products and why it is relevant to this blog post.

What other media/videos/souces/links will I include giving more value to the blog post. Who is an expert in this area? Give details below:

BLOG POST TEMPLATE

Title ideas (use keyword research)

Overall point of blog post (to inform, solve a problem, educate, entertain) - give more detail here

What are 3- 5 points that need answering in this blog post (use google, quora, questions from forums etc)

Is there a particular product/s I want to promote or a website I want to send traffic to? Give details of benefits of those products and why it is relevant to this blog post.

What other media/videos/souces/links will I include giving more value to the blog post. Who is an expert in this area? Give details below:

BLOG POST TEMPLATE

Title ideas (use keyword research)

Overall point of blog post (to inform, solve a problem, educate, entertain) - give more detail here

What are 3- 5 points that need answering in this blog post (use google, quora, questions from forums etc)

Is there a particular product/s I want to promote or a website I want to send traffic to? Give details of benefits of those products and why it is relevant to this blog post.

What other media/videos/souces/links will I include giving more value to the blog post. Who is an expert in this area? Give details below:

BLOG POST TEMPLATE

Title ideas (use keyword research)

Overall point of blog post (to inform, solve a problem, educate, entertain) - give more detail here

What are 3- 5 points that need answering in this blog post (use google, quora, questions from forums etc)

Is there a particular product/s I want to promote or a website I want to send traffic to? Give details of benefits of those products and why it is relevant to this blog post.

What other media/videos/souces/links will I include giving more value to the blog post. Who is an expert in this area? Give details below:

BLOG POST TEMPLATE

Title ideas (use keyword research)

Overall point of blog post (to inform, solve a problem, educate, entertain) - give more detail here

What are 3- 5 points that need answering in this blog post (use google, quora, questions from forums etc)

Is there a particular product/s I want to promote or a website I want to send traffic to? Give details of benefits of those products and why it is relevant to this blog post.

What other media/videos/souces/links will I include giving more value to the blog post. Who is an expert in this area? Give details below:

BLOG POST TEMPLATE

Title ideas (use keyword research)

Overall point of blog post (to inform, solve a problem, educate, entertain) - give more detail here

What are 3- 5 points that need answering in this blog post (use google, quora, questions from forums etc)

Is there a particular product/s I want to promote or a website I want to send traffic to? Give details of benefits of those products and why it is relevant to this blog post.

What other media/videos/souces/links will I include giving more value to the blog post. Who is an expert in this area? Give details below:

BLOG POST TEMPLATE

Title ideas (use keyword research)

Overall point of blog post (to inform, solve a problem, educate, entertain) - give more detail here

What are 3- 5 points that need answering in this blog post (use google, quora, questions from forums etc)

Is there a particular product/s I want to promote or a website I want to send traffic to? Give details of benefits of those products and why it is relevant to this blog post.

What other media/videos/souces/links will I include giving more value to the blog post. Who is an expert in this area? Give details below:

BLOG POST TEMPLATE

Title ideas (use keyword research)

Overall point of blog post (to inform, solve a problem, educate, entertain) - give more detail here

What are 3- 5 points that need answering in this blog post (use google, quora, questions from forums etc)

Is there a particular product/s I want to promote or a website I want to send traffic to? Give details of benefits of those products and why it is relevant to this blog post.

What other media/videos/souces/links will I include giving more value to the blog post. Who is an expert in this area? Give details below:

BLOG POST TEMPLATE

Title ideas (use keyword research)

Overall point of blog post (to inform, solve a problem, educate, entertain) - give more detail here

What are 3- 5 points that need answering in this blog post (use google, quora, questions from forums etc)

Is there a particular product/s I want to promote or a website I want to send traffic to? Give details of benefits of those products and why it is relevant to this blog post.

What other media/videos/souces/links will I include giving more value to the blog post. Who is an expert in this area? Give details below:

BLOG POST TEMPLATE

Title ideas (use keyword research)

Overall point of blog post (to inform, solve a problem, educate, entertain) - give more detail here

What are 3- 5 points that need answering in this blog post (use google, quora, questions from forums etc)

Is there a particular product/s I want to promote or a website I want to send traffic to? Give details of benefits of those products and why it is relevant to this blog post.

What other media/videos/souces/links will I include giving more value to the blog post. Who is an expert in this area? Give details below:

BLOG POST TEMPLATE

Title ideas (use keyword research)

Overall point of blog post (to inform, solve a problem, educate, entertain) - give more detail here

What are 3- 5 points that need answering in this blog post (use google, quora, questions from forums etc)

Is there a particular product/s I want to promote or a website I want to send traffic to? Give details of benefits of those products and why it is relevant to this blog post.

What other media/videos/souces/links will I include giving more value to the blog post. Who is an expert in this area? Give details below:

BLOG POST TEMPLATE

Title ideas (use keyword research)

Overall point of blog post (to inform, solve a problem, educate, entertain) - give more detail here

What are 3- 5 points that need answering in this blog post (use google, quora, questions from forums etc)

Is there a particular product/s I want to promote or a website I want to send traffic to? Give details of benefits of those products and why it is relevant to this blog post.

What other media/videos/souces/links will I include giving more value to the blog post. Who is an expert in this area? Give details below:

BLOG POST TEMPLATE

Title ideas (use keyword research)

Overall point of blog post (to inform, solve a problem, educate, entertain) - give more detail here

What are 3- 5 points that need answering in this blog post (use google, quora, questions from forums etc)

Is there a particular product/s I want to promote or a website I want to send traffic to? Give details of benefits of those products and why it is relevant to this blog post.

What other media/videos/souces/links will I include giving more value to the blog post. Who is an expert in this area? Give details below:

BLOG POST TEMPLATE

Title ideas (use keyword research)

Overall point of blog post (to inform, solve a problem, educate, entertain) - give more detail here

What are 3- 5 points that need answering in this blog post (use google, quora, questions from forums etc)

Is there a particular product/s I want to promote or a website I want to send traffic to? Give details of benefits of those products and why it is relevant to this blog post.

What other media/videos/souces/links will I include giving more value to the blog post. Who is an expert in this area? Give details below:

BLOG POST TEMPLATE

Title ideas (use keyword research)

Overall point of blog post (to inform, solve a problem, educate, entertain) - give more detail here

What are 3- 5 points that need answering in this blog post (use google, quora, questions from forums etc)

Is there a particular product/s I want to promote or a website I want to send traffic to? Give details of benefits of those products and why it is relevant to this blog post.

What other media/videos/souces/links will I include giving more value to the blog post. Who is an expert in this area? Give details below:

BLOG POST TEMPLATE

Title ideas (use keyword research)

Overall point of blog post (to inform, solve a problem, educate, entertain) - give more detail here

What are 3- 5 points that need answering in this blog post (use google, quora, questions from forums etc)

Is there a particular product/s I want to promote or a website I want to send traffic to? Give details of benefits of those products and why it is relevant to this blog post.

What other media/videos/souces/links will I include giving more value to the blog post. Who is an expert in this area? Give details below:

BLOG POST TEMPLATE

Title ideas (use keyword research)

Overall point of blog post (to inform, solve a problem, educate, entertain) - give more detail here

What are 3- 5 points that need answering in this blog post (use google, quora, questions from forums etc)

Is there a particular product/s I want to promote or a website I want to send traffic to? Give details of benefits of those products and why it is relevant to this blog post.

What other media/videos/souces/links will I include giving more value to the blog post. Who is an expert in this area? Give details below:

BLOG POST TEMPLATE

Title ideas (use keyword research)

Overall point of blog post (to inform, solve a problem, educate, entertain) - give more detail here

What are 3- 5 points that need answering in this blog post (use google, quora, questions from forums etc)

Is there a particular product/s I want to promote or a website I want to send traffic to? Give details of benefits of those products and why it is relevant to this blog post.

What other media/videos/souces/links will I include giving more value to the blog post. Who is an expert in this area? Give details below:

BLOG POST TEMPLATE

Title ideas (use keyword research)

Overall point of blog post (to inform, solve a problem, educate, entertain) - give more detail here

What are 3- 5 points that need answering in this blog post (use google, quora, questions from forums etc)

Is there a particular product/s I want to promote or a website I want to send traffic to? Give details of benefits of those products and why it is relevant to this blog post.

What other media/videos/souces/links will I include giving more value to the blog post. Who is an expert in this area? Give details below:

BLOG POST TEMPLATE

Title ideas (use keyword research)

Overall point of blog post (to inform, solve a problem, educate, entertain) - give more detail here

What are 3- 5 points that need answering in this blog post (use google, quora, questions from forums etc)

Is there a particular product/s I want to promote or a website I want to send traffic to? Give details of benefits of those products and why it is relevant to this blog post.

What other media/videos/souces/links will I include giving more value to the blog post. Who is an expert in this area? Give details below:

BLOG POST TEMPLATE

Title ideas (use keyword research)

Overall point of blog post (to inform, solve a problem, educate, entertain) - give more detail here

What are 3- 5 points that need answering in this blog post (use google, quora, questions from forums etc)

Is there a particular product/s I want to promote or a website I want to send traffic to? Give details of benefits of those products and why it is relevant to this blog post.

What other media/videos/souces/links will I include giving more value to the blog post. Who is an expert in this area? Give details below:

BLOG POST TEMPLATE

Title ideas (use keyword research)

Overall point of blog post (to inform, solve a problem, educate, entertain) - give more detail here

What are 3- 5 points that need answering in this blog post (use google, quora, questions from forums etc)

Is there a particular product/s I want to promote or a website I want to send traffic to? Give details of benefits of those products and why it is relevant to this blog post.

What other media/videos/souces/links will I include giving more value to the blog post. Who is an expert in this area? Give details below:

BLOG POST TEMPLATE

Title ideas (use keyword research)

Overall point of blog post (to inform, solve a problem, educate, entertain) - give more detail here

What are 3- 5 points that need answering in this blog post (use google, quora, questions from forums etc)

Is there a particular product/s I want to promote or a website I want to send traffic to? Give details of benefits of those products and why it is relevant to this blog post.

What other media/videos/souces/links will I include giving more value to the blog post. Who is an expert in this area? Give details below:

BLOG POST TEMPLATE

Title ideas (use keyword research)

Overall point of blog post (to inform, solve a problem, educate, entertain) - give more detail here

What are 3- 5 points that need answering in this blog post (use google, quora, questions from forums etc)

Is there a particular product/s I want to promote or a website I want to send traffic to? Give details of benefits of those products and why it is relevant to this blog post.

What other media/videos/souces/links will I include giving more value to the blog post. Who is an expert in this area? Give details below:

BLOG POST TEMPLATE

Title ideas (use keyword research)

Overall point of blog post (to inform, solve a problem, educate, entertain) - give more detail here

What are 3- 5 points that need answering in this blog post (use google, quora, questions from forums etc)

Is there a particular product/s I want to promote or a website I want to send traffic to? Give details of benefits of those products and why it is relevant to this blog post.

What other media/videos/souces/links will I include giving more value to the blog post. Who is an expert in this area? Give details below:

BLOG POST TEMPLATE

Title ideas (use keyword research)

Overall point of blog post (to inform, solve a problem, educate, entertain) - give more detail here

What are 3- 5 points that need answering in this blog post (use google, quora, questions from forums etc)

Is there a particular product/s I want to promote or a website I want to send traffic to? Give details of benefits of those products and why it is relevant to this blog post.

What other media/videos/souces/links will I include giving more value to the blog post. Who is an expert in this area? Give details below:

BLOG POST TEMPLATE

Title ideas (use keyword research)

Overall point of blog post (to inform, solve a problem, educate, entertain) - give more detail here

What are 3- 5 points that need answering in this blog post (use google, quora, questions from forums etc)

Is there a particular product/s I want to promote or a website I want to send traffic to? Give details of benefits of those products and why it is relevant to this blog post.

What other media/videos/souces/links will I include giving more value to the blog post. Who is an expert in this area? Give details below:

BLOG POST TEMPLATE

Title ideas (use keyword research)

Overall point of blog post (to inform, solve a problem, educate, entertain) - give more detail here

What are 3- 5 points that need answering in this blog post (use google, quora, questions from forums etc)

Is there a particular product/s I want to promote or a website I want to send traffic to? Give details of benefits of those products and why it is relevant to this blog post.

What other media/videos/souces/links will I include giving more value to the blog post. Who is an expert in this area? Give details below:

BLOG POST TEMPLATE

Title ideas (use keyword research)

Overall point of blog post (to inform, solve a problem, educate, entertain) - give more detail here

What are 3- 5 points that need answering in this blog post (use google, quora, questions from forums etc)

Is there a particular product/s I want to promote or a website I want to send traffic to? Give details of benefits of those products and why it is relevant to this blog post.

What other media/videos/souces/links will I include giving more value to the blog post. Who is an expert in this area? Give details below:

BLOG POST TEMPLATE

Title ideas (use keyword research)

Overall point of blog post (to inform, solve a problem, educate, entertain) - give more detail here

What are 3- 5 points that need answering in this blog post (use google, quora, questions from forums etc)

Is there a particular product/s I want to promote or a website I want to send traffic to? Give details of benefits of those products and why it is relevant to this blog post.

What other media/videos/souces/links will I include giving more value to the blog post. Who is an expert in this area? Give details below:

BLOG POST TEMPLATE

Title ideas (use keyword research)

Overall point of blog post (to inform, solve a problem, educate, entertain) - give more detail here

What are 3- 5 points that need answering in this blog post (use google, quora, questions from forums etc)

Is there a particular product/s I want to promote or a website I want to send traffic to? Give details of benefits of those products and why it is relevant to this blog post.

What other media/videos/souces/links will I include giving more value to the blog post. Who is an expert in this area? Give details below:

BLOG POST TEMPLATE

Title ideas (use keyword research)

Overall point of blog post (to inform, solve a problem, educate, entertain) - give more detail here

What are 3- 5 points that need answering in this blog post (use google, quora, questions from forums etc)

Is there a particular product/s I want to promote or a website I want to send traffic to? Give details of benefits of those products and why it is relevant to this blog post.

What other media/videos/souces/links will I include giving more value to the blog post. Who is an expert in this area? Give details below:

BLOG POST TEMPLATE

Title ideas (use keyword research)

Overall point of blog post (to inform, solve a problem, educate, entertain) - give more detail here

What are 3- 5 points that need answering in this blog post (use google, quora, questions from forums etc)

Is there a particular product/s I want to promote or a website I want to send traffic to? Give details of benefits of those products and why it is relevant to this blog post.

What other media/videos/souces/links will I include giving more value to the blog post. Who is an expert in this area? Give details below:

BLOG POST TEMPLATE

Title ideas (use keyword research)

Overall point of blog post (to inform, solve a problem, educate, entertain) - give more detail here

What are 3- 5 points that need answering in this blog post (use google, quora, questions from forums etc)

Is there a particular product/s I want to promote or a website I want to send traffic to? Give details of benefits of those products and why it is relevant to this blog post.

What other media/videos/souces/links will I include giving more value to the blog post. Who is an expert in this area? Give details below:

BLOG POST TEMPLATE

Title ideas (use keyword research)

Overall point of blog post (to inform, solve a problem, educate, entertain) - give more detail here

What are 3- 5 points that need answering in this blog post (use google, quora, questions from forums etc)

Is there a particular product/s I want to promote or a website I want to send traffic to? Give details of benefits of those products and why it is relevant to this blog post.

What other media/videos/souces/links will I include giving more value to the blog post. Who is an expert in this area? Give details below:

BLOG POST TEMPLATE

Title ideas (use keyword research)

Overall point of blog post (to inform, solve a problem, educate, entertain) - give more detail here

What are 3- 5 points that need answering in this blog post (use google, quora, questions from forums etc)

Is there a particular product/s I want to promote or a website I want to send traffic to? Give details of benefits of those products and why it is relevant to this blog post.

What other media/videos/souces/links will I include giving more value to the blog post. Who is an expert in this area? Give details below:

BLOG POST TEMPLATE

Title ideas (use keyword research)

Overall point of blog post (to inform, solve a problem, educate, entertain) - give more detail here

What are 3- 5 points that need answering in this blog post (use google, quora, questions from forums etc)

Is there a particular product/s I want to promote or a website I want to send traffic to? Give details of benefits of those products and why it is relevant to this blog post.

What other media/videos/souces/links will I include giving more value to the blog post. Who is an expert in this area? Give details below:

BLOG POST TEMPLATE

Title ideas (use keyword research)

Overall point of blog post (to inform, solve a problem, educate, entertain) - give more detail here

What are 3- 5 points that need answering in this blog post (use google, quora, questions from forums etc)

Is there a particular product/s I want to promote or a website I want to send traffic to? Give details of benefits of those products and why it is relevant to this blog post.

What other media/videos/souces/links will I include giving more value to the blog post. Who is an expert in this area? Give details below:

BLOG POST TEMPLATE

Title ideas (use keyword research)

Overall point of blog post (to inform, solve a problem, educate, entertain) - give more detail here

What are 3- 5 points that need answering in this blog post (use google, quora, questions from forums etc)

Is there a particular product/s I want to promote or a website I want to send traffic to? Give details of benefits of those products and why it is relevant to this blog post.

What other media/videos/souces/links will I include giving more value to the blog post. Who is an expert in this area? Give details below:

BLOG POST TEMPLATE

Title ideas (use keyword research)

Overall point of blog post (to inform, solve a problem, educate, entertain) - give more detail here

What are 3- 5 points that need answering in this blog post (use google, quora, questions from forums etc)

Is there a particular product/s I want to promote or a website I want to send traffic to? Give details of benefits of those products and why it is relevant to this blog post.

What other media/videos/souces/links will I include giving more value to the blog post. Who is an expert in this area? Give details below:

BLOG POST TEMPLATE

Title ideas (use keyword research)

Overall point of blog post (to inform, solve a problem, educate, entertain) - give more detail here

What are 3- 5 points that need answering in this blog post (use google, quora, questions from forums etc)

Is there a particular product/s I want to promote or a website I want to send traffic to? Give details of benefits of those products and why it is relevant to this blog post.

What other media/videos/souces/links will I include giving more value to the blog post. Who is an expert in this area? Give details below:

BLOG POST TEMPLATE

Title ideas (use keyword research)

Overall point of blog post (to inform, solve a problem, educate, entertain) - give more detail here

What are 3- 5 points that need answering in this blog post (use google, quora, questions from forums etc)

Is there a particular product/s I want to promote or a website I want to send traffic to? Give details of benefits of those products and why it is relevant to this blog post.

What other media/videos/souces/links will I include giving more value to the blog post. Who is an expert in this area? Give details below:

BLOG POST TEMPLATE

Title ideas (use keyword research)

Overall point of blog post (to inform, solve a problem, educate, entertain) - give more detail here

What are 3- 5 points that need answering in this blog post (use google, quora, questions from forums etc)

Is there a particular product/s I want to promote or a website I want to send traffic to? Give details of benefits of those products and why it is relevant to this blog post.

What other media/videos/souces/links will I include giving more value to the blog post. Who is an expert in this area? Give details below:

BLOG POST TEMPLATE

Title ideas (use keyword research)

Overall point of blog post (to inform, solve a problem, educate, entertain) - give more detail here

What are 3- 5 points that need answering in this blog post (use google, quora, questions from forums etc)

Is there a particular product/s I want to promote or a website I want to send traffic to? Give details of benefits of those products and why it is relevant to this blog post.

What other media/videos/souces/links will I include giving more value to the blog post. Who is an expert in this area? Give details below:

BLOG POST TEMPLATE

Title ideas (use keyword research)

Overall point of blog post (to inform, solve a problem, educate, entertain) - give more detail here

What are 3- 5 points that need answering in this blog post (use google, quora, questions from forums etc)

Is there a particular product/s I want to promote or a website I want to send traffic to? Give details of benefits of those products and why it is relevant to this blog post.

What other media/videos/souces/links will I include giving more value to the blog post. Who is an expert in this area? Give details below:

BLOG POST TEMPLATE

Title ideas (use keyword research)

Overall point of blog post (to inform, solve a problem, educate, entertain) - give more detail here

What are 3- 5 points that need answering in this blog post (use google, quora, questions from forums etc)

Is there a particular product/s I want to promote or a website I want to send traffic to? Give details of benefits of those products and why it is relevant to this blog post.

What other media/videos/souces/links will I include giving more value to the blog post. Who is an expert in this area? Give details below:

BLOG POST TEMPLATE

Title ideas (use keyword research)

Overall point of blog post (to inform, solve a problem, educate, entertain) - give more detail here

What are 3- 5 points that need answering in this blog post (use google, quora, questions from forums etc)

Is there a particular product/s I want to promote or a website I want to send traffic to? Give details of benefits of those products and why it is relevant to this blog post.

What other media/videos/souces/links will I include giving more value to the blog post. Who is an expert in this area? Give details below:

BLOG POST TEMPLATE

Title ideas (use keyword research)

Overall point of blog post (to inform, solve a problem, educate, entertain) - give more detail here

What are 3- 5 points that need answering in this blog post (use google, quora, questions from forums etc)

Is there a particular product/s I want to promote or a website I want to send traffic to? Give details of benefits of those products and why it is relevant to this blog post.

What other media/videos/souces/links will I include giving more value to the blog post. Who is an expert in this area? Give details below:

BLOG POST TEMPLATE

Title ideas (use keyword research)

Overall point of blog post (to inform, solve a problem, educate, entertain) - give more detail here

What are 3- 5 points that need answering in this blog post (use google, quora, questions from forums etc)

Is there a particular product/s I want to promote or a website I want to send traffic to? Give details of benefits of those products and why it is relevant to this blog post.

What other media/videos/souces/links will I include giving more value to the blog post. Who is an expert in this area? Give details below:

BLOG POST TEMPLATE

Title ideas (use keyword research)

Overall point of blog post (to inform, solve a problem, educate, entertain) - give more detail here

What are 3- 5 points that need answering in this blog post (use google, quora, questions from forums etc)

Is there a particular product/s I want to promote or a website I want to send traffic to? Give details of benefits of those products and why it is relevant to this blog post.

What other media/videos/souces/links will I include giving more value to the blog post. Who is an expert in this area? Give details below:

BLOG POST TEMPLATE

Title ideas (use keyword research)

Overall point of blog post (to inform, solve a problem, educate, entertain) - give more detail here

What are 3- 5 points that need answering in this blog post (use google, quora, questions from forums etc)

Is there a particular product/s I want to promote or a website I want to send traffic to? Give details of benefits of those products and why it is relevant to this blog post.

What other media/videos/souces/links will I include giving more value to the blog post. Who is an expert in this area? Give details below:

BLOG POST TEMPLATE

Title ideas (use keyword research)

Overall point of blog post (to inform, solve a problem, educate, entertain) - give more detail here

What are 3- 5 points that need answering in this blog post (use google, quora, questions from forums etc)

Is there a particular product/s I want to promote or a website I want to send traffic to? Give details of benefits of those products and why it is relevant to this blog post.

What other media/videos/souces/links will I include giving more value to the blog post. Who is an expert in this area? Give details below:

BLOG POST TEMPLATE

Title ideas (use keyword research)

Overall point of blog post (to inform, solve a problem, educate, entertain) - give more detail here

What are 3- 5 points that need answering in this blog post (use google, quora, questions from forums etc)

Is there a particular product/s I want to promote or a website I want to send traffic to? Give details of benefits of those products and why it is relevant to this blog post.

What other media/videos/souces/links will I include giving more value to the blog post. Who is an expert in this area? Give details below:

BLOG POST TEMPLATE

Title ideas (use keyword research)

Overall point of blog post (to inform, solve a problem, educate, entertain) - give more detail here

What are 3- 5 points that need answering in this blog post (use google, quora, questions from forums etc)

Is there a particular product/s I want to promote or a website I want to send traffic to? Give details of benefits of those products and why it is relevant to this blog post.

What other media/videos/souces/links will I include giving more value to the blog post. Who is an expert in this area? Give details below:

BLOG POST TEMPLATE

Title ideas (use keyword research)

Overall point of blog post (to inform, solve a problem, educate, entertain) - give more detail here

What are 3- 5 points that need answering in this blog post (use google, quora, questions from forums etc)

Is there a particular product/s I want to promote or a website I want to send traffic to? Give details of benefits of those products and why it is relevant to this blog post.

What other media/videos/souces/links will I include giving more value to the blog post. Who is an expert in this area? Give details below:

BLOG POST TEMPLATE

Title ideas (use keyword research)

Overall point of blog post (to inform, solve a problem, educate, entertain) - give more detail here

What are 3- 5 points that need answering in this blog post (use google, quora, questions from forums etc)

Is there a particular product/s I want to promote or a website I want to send traffic to? Give details of benefits of those products and why it is relevant to this blog post.

What other media/videos/souces/links will I include giving more value to the blog post. Who is an expert in this area? Give details below:

BLOG POST TEMPLATE

Title ideas (use keyword research)

Overall point of blog post (to inform, solve a problem, educate, entertain) - give more detail here

What are 3- 5 points that need answering in this blog post (use google, quora, questions from forums etc)

Is there a particular product/s I want to promote or a website I want to send traffic to? Give details of benefits of those products and why it is relevant to this blog post.

What other media/videos/souces/links will I include giving more value to the blog post. Who is an expert in this area? Give details below:

BLOG POST TEMPLATE

Title ideas (use keyword research)

Overall point of blog post (to inform, solve a problem, educate, entertain) - give more detail here

What are 3- 5 points that need answering in this blog post (use google, quora, questions from forums etc)

Is there a particular product/s I want to promote or a website I want to send traffic to? Give details of benefits of those products and why it is relevant to this blog post.

What other media/videos/souces/links will I include giving more value to the blog post. Who is an expert in this area? Give details below:

BLOG POST TEMPLATE

Title ideas (use keyword research)

Overall point of blog post (to inform, solve a problem, educate, entertain) - give more detail here

What are 3- 5 points that need answering in this blog post (use google, quora, questions from forums etc)

Is there a particular product/s I want to promote or a website I want to send traffic to? Give details of benefits of those products and why it is relevant to this blog post.

What other media/videos/souces/links will I include giving more value to the blog post. Who is an expert in this area? Give details below:

BLOG POST TEMPLATE

Title ideas (use keyword research)

Overall point of blog post (to inform, solve a problem, educate, entertain) - give more detail here

What are 3- 5 points that need answering in this blog post (use google, quora, questions from forums etc)

Is there a particular product/s I want to promote or a website I want to send traffic to? Give details of benefits of those products and why it is relevant to this blog post.

What other media/videos/souces/links will I include giving more value to the blog post. Who is an expert in this area? Give details below:

BLOG POST TEMPLATE

Title ideas (use keyword research)

Overall point of blog post (to inform, solve a problem, educate, entertain) - give more detail here

What are 3- 5 points that need answering in this blog post (use google, quora, questions from forums etc)

Is there a particular product/s I want to promote or a website I want to send traffic to? Give details of benefits of those products and why it is relevant to this blog post.

What other media/videos/souces/links will I include giving more value to the blog post. Who is an expert in this area? Give details below:

BLOG POST TEMPLATE

Title ideas (use keyword research)

Overall point of blog post (to inform, solve a problem, educate, entertain) - give more detail here

What are 3- 5 points that need answering in this blog post (use google, quora, questions from forums etc)

Is there a particular product/s I want to promote or a website I want to send traffic to? Give details of benefits of those products and why it is relevant to this blog post.

What other media/videos/souces/links will I include giving more value to the blog post. Who is an expert in this area? Give details below:

BLOG POST TEMPLATE

Title ideas (use keyword research)

Overall point of blog post (to inform, solve a problem, educate, entertain) - give more detail here

What are 3- 5 points that need answering in this blog post (use google, quora, questions from forums etc)

Is there a particular product/s I want to promote or a website I want to send traffic to? Give details of benefits of those products and why it is relevant to this blog post.

What other media/videos/souces/links will I include giving more value to the blog post. Who is an expert in this area? Give details below:

BLOG POST TEMPLATE

Title ideas (use keyword research)

Overall point of blog post (to inform, solve a problem, educate, entertain) - give more detail here

What are 3- 5 points that need answering in this blog post (use google, quora, questions from forums etc)

Is there a particular product/s I want to promote or a website I want to send traffic to? Give details of benefits of those products and why it is relevant to this blog post.

What other media/videos/souces/links will I include giving more value to the blog post. Who is an expert in this area? Give details below:

BLOG POST TEMPLATE

Title ideas (use keyword research)

Overall point of blog post (to inform, solve a problem, educate, entertain) - give more detail here

What are 3- 5 points that need answering in this blog post (use google, quora, questions from forums etc)

Is there a particular product/s I want to promote or a website I want to send traffic to? Give details of benefits of those products and why it is relevant to this blog post.

What other media/videos/souces/links will I include giving more value to the blog post. Who is an expert in this area? Give details below:

BLOG POST TEMPLATE

Title ideas (use keyword research)

Overall point of blog post (to inform, solve a problem, educate, entertain) - give more detail here

What are 3- 5 points that need answering in this blog post (use google, quora, questions from forums etc)

Is there a particular product/s I want to promote or a website I want to send traffic to? Give details of benefits of those products and why it is relevant to this blog post.

What other media/videos/souces/links will I include giving more value to the blog post. Who is an expert in this area? Give details below:

BLOG POST TEMPLATE

Title ideas (use keyword research)

Overall point of blog post (to inform, solve a problem, educate, entertain) - give more detail here

What are 3- 5 points that need answering in this blog post (use google, quora, questions from forums etc)

Is there a particular product/s I want to promote or a website I want to send traffic to? Give details of benefits of those products and why it is relevant to this blog post.

What other media/videos/souces/links will I include giving more value to the blog post. Who is an expert in this area? Give details below:

HackneyandJones.com

BLOG POST TEMPLATE

Title ideas (use keyword research)

Overall point of blog post (to inform, solve a problem, educate, entertain) - give more detail here

What are 3- 5 points that need answering in this blog post (use google, quora, questions from forums etc)

Is there a particular product/s I want to promote or a website I want to send traffic to? Give details of benefits of those products and why it is relevant to this blog post.

What other media/videos/souces/links will I include giving more value to the blog post. Who is an expert in this area? Give details below:

BLOG POST TEMPLATE

Title ideas (use keyword research)

Overall point of blog post (to inform, solve a problem, educate, entertain) - give more detail here

What are 3- 5 points that need answering in this blog post (use google, quora, questions from forums etc)

Is there a particular product/s I want to promote or a website I want to send traffic to? Give details of benefits of those products and why it is relevant to this blog post.

What other media/videos/souces/links will I include giving more value to the blog post. Who is an expert in this area? Give details below:

BLOG POST TEMPLATE

Title ideas (use keyword research)

Overall point of blog post (to inform, solve a problem, educate, entertain) - give more detail here

What are 3- 5 points that need answering in this blog post (use google, quora, questions from forums etc)

Is there a particular product/s I want to promote or a website I want to send traffic to? Give details of benefits of those products and why it is relevant to this blog post.

What other media/videos/souces/links will I include giving more value to the blog post. Who is an expert in this area? Give details below:

BLOG POST TEMPLATE

Title ideas (use keyword research)

Overall point of blog post (to inform, solve a problem, educate, entertain) - give more detail here

What are 3- 5 points that need answering in this blog post (use google, quora, questions from forums etc)

Is there a particular product/s I want to promote or a website I want to send traffic to? Give details of benefits of those products and why it is relevant to this blog post.

What other media/videos/souces/links will I include giving more value to the blog post. Who is an expert in this area? Give details below:

BLOG POST TEMPLATE

Title ideas (use keyword research)

Overall point of blog post (to inform, solve a problem, educate, entertain) - give more detail here

What are 3- 5 points that need answering in this blog post (use google, quora, questions from forums etc)

Is there a particular product/s I want to promote or a website I want to send traffic to? Give details of benefits of those products and why it is relevant to this blog post.

What other media/videos/souces/links will I include giving more value to the blog post. Who is an expert in this area? Give details below:

HackneyandJones.com

BLOG POST TEMPLATE

Title ideas (use keyword research)

Overall point of blog post (to inform, solve a problem, educate, entertain) - give more detail here

What are 3- 5 points that need answering in this blog post (use google, quora, questions from forums etc)

Is there a particular product/s I want to promote or a website I want to send traffic to? Give details of benefits of those products and why it is relevant to this blog post.

What other media/videos/souces/links will I include giving more value to the blog post. Who is an expert in this area? Give details below:

BLOG POST TEMPLATE

Title ideas (use keyword research)

Overall point of blog post (to inform, solve a problem, educate, entertain) - give more detail here

What are 3- 5 points that need answering in this blog post (use google, quora, questions from forums etc)

Is there a particular product/s I want to promote or a website I want to send traffic to? Give details of benefits of those products and why it is relevant to this blog post.

What other media/videos/souces/links will I include giving more value to the blog post. Who is an expert in this area? Give details below:

BLOG POST TEMPLATE

Title ideas (use keyword research)

Overall point of blog post (to inform, solve a problem, educate, entertain) - give more detail here

What are 3- 5 points that need answering in this blog post (use google, quora, questions from forums etc)

Is there a particular product/s I want to promote or a website I want to send traffic to? Give details of benefits of those products and why it is relevant to this blog post.

What other media/videos/souces/links will I include giving more value to the blog post. Who is an expert in this area? Give details below:

BLOG POST TEMPLATE

Title ideas (use keyword research)

Overall point of blog post (to inform, solve a problem, educate, entertain) - give more detail here

What are 3- 5 points that need answering in this blog post (use google, quora, questions from forums etc)

Is there a particular product/s I want to promote or a website I want to send traffic to? Give details of benefits of those products and why it is relevant to this blog post.

What other media/videos/souces/links will I include giving more value to the blog post. Who is an expert in this area? Give details below:

BLOG POST TEMPLATE

Title ideas (use keyword research)

Overall point of blog post (to inform, solve a problem, educate, entertain) - give more detail here

What are 3- 5 points that need answering in this blog post (use google, quora, questions from forums etc)

Is there a particular product/s I want to promote or a website I want to send traffic to? Give details of benefits of those products and why it is relevant to this blog post.

What other media/videos/souces/links will I include giving more value to the blog post. Who is an expert in this area? Give details below:

HackneyandJones.com

BLOG POST TEMPLATE

Title ideas (use keyword research)

Overall point of blog post (to inform, solve a problem, educate, entertain) - give more detail here

What are 3- 5 points that need answering in this blog post (use google, quora, questions from forums etc)

Is there a particular product/s I want to promote or a website I want to send traffic to? Give details of benefits of those products and why it is relevant to this blog post.

What other media/videos/souces/links will I include giving more value to the blog post. Who is an expert in this area? Give details below:

HackneyandJones.com

BLOG POST TEMPLATE

Title ideas (use keyword research)

Overall point of blog post (to inform, solve a problem, educate, entertain) - give more detail here

What are 3- 5 points that need answering in this blog post (use google, quora, questions from forums etc)

Is there a particular product/s I want to promote or a website I want to send traffic to? Give details of benefits of those products and why it is relevant to this blog post.

What other media/videos/souces/links will I include giving more value to the blog post. Who is an expert in this area? Give details below:

BLOG POST TEMPLATE

Title ideas (use keyword research)

Overall point of blog post (to inform, solve a problem, educate, entertain) - give more detail here

What are 3- 5 points that need answering in this blog post (use google, quora, questions from forums etc)

Is there a particular product/s I want to promote or a website I want to send traffic to? Give details of benefits of those products and why it is relevant to this blog post.

What other media/videos/souces/links will I include giving more value to the blog post. Who is an expert in this area? Give details below:

BLOG POST TEMPLATE

Title ideas (use keyword research)

Overall point of blog post (to inform, solve a problem, educate, entertain) - give more detail here

What are 3- 5 points that need answering in this blog post (use google, quora, questions from forums etc)

Is there a particular product/s I want to promote or a website I want to send traffic to? Give details of benefits of those products and why it is relevant to this blog post.

What other media/videos/souces/links will I include giving more value to the blog post. Who is an expert in this area? Give details below:

BLOG POST TEMPLATE

Title ideas (use keyword research)

Overall point of blog post (to inform, solve a problem, educate, entertain) - give more detail here

What are 3- 5 points that need answering in this blog post (use google, quora, questions from forums etc)

Is there a particular product/s I want to promote or a website I want to send traffic to? Give details of benefits of those products and why it is relevant to this blog post.

What other media/videos/souces/links will I include giving more value to the blog post. Who is an expert in this area? Give details below:

BLOG POST TEMPLATE

Title ideas (use keyword research)

Overall point of blog post (to inform, solve a problem, educate, entertain) - give more detail here

What are 3- 5 points that need answering in this blog post (use google, quora, questions from forums etc)

Is there a particular product/s I want to promote or a website I want to send traffic to? Give details of benefits of those products and why it is relevant to this blog post.

What other media/videos/souces/links will I include giving more value to the blog post. Who is an expert in this area? Give details below:

BLOG POST TEMPLATE

Title ideas (use keyword research)

Overall point of blog post (to inform, solve a problem, educate, entertain) - give more detail here

What are 3- 5 points that need answering in this blog post (use google, quora, questions from forums etc)

Is there a particular product/s I want to promote or a website I want to send traffic to? Give details of benefits of those products and why it is relevant to this blog post.

What other media/videos/souces/links will I include giving more value to the blog post. Who is an expert in this area? Give details below:

BLOG POST TEMPLATE

Title ideas (use keyword research)

Overall point of blog post (to inform, solve a problem, educate, entertain) - give more detail here

What are 3- 5 points that need answering in this blog post (use google, quora, questions from forums etc)

Is there a particular product/s I want to promote or a website I want to send traffic to? Give details of benefits of those products and why it is relevant to this blog post.

What other media/videos/souces/links will I include giving more value to the blog post. Who is an expert in this area? Give details below:

BLOG POST TEMPLATE

Title ideas (use keyword research)

Overall point of blog post (to inform, solve a problem, educate, entertain) - give more detail here

What are 3- 5 points that need answering in this blog post (use google, quora, questions from forums etc)

Is there a particular product/s I want to promote or a website I want to send traffic to? Give details of benefits of those products and why it is relevant to this blog post.

What other media/videos/souces/links will I include giving more value to the blog post. Who is an expert in this area? Give details below:

BLOG POST TEMPLATE

Title ideas (use keyword research)

Overall point of blog post (to inform, solve a problem, educate, entertain) - give more detail here

What are 3- 5 points that need answering in this blog post (use google, quora, questions from forums etc)

Is there a particular product/s I want to promote or a website I want to send traffic to? Give details of benefits of those products and why it is relevant to this blog post.

What other media/videos/souces/links will I include giving more value to the blog post. Who is an expert in this area? Give details below:

BLOG POST TEMPLATE

Title ideas (use keyword research)

Overall point of blog post (to inform, solve a problem, educate, entertain) - give more detail here

What are 3- 5 points that need answering in this blog post (use google, quora, questions from forums etc)

Is there a particular product/s I want to promote or a website I want to send traffic to? Give details of benefits of those products and why it is relevant to this blog post.

What other media/videos/souces/links will I include giving more value to the blog post. Who is an expert in this area? Give details below:

BLOG POST TEMPLATE

Title ideas (use keyword research)

Overall point of blog post (to inform, solve a problem, educate, entertain) - give more detail here

What are 3- 5 points that need answering in this blog post (use google, quora, questions from forums etc)

Is there a particular product/s I want to promote or a website I want to send traffic to? Give details of benefits of those products and why it is relevant to this blog post.

What other media/videos/souces/links will I include giving more value to the blog post. Who is an expert in this area? Give details below:

Want a Freebie?

VISIT

HACKNEYANDJONES.COM

NOW

Free fiction books, non-fiction and kids
activity sheets.

Printed in Great Britain
by Amazon

22094641R00057